OXYGEN II

Poems

BETH BROWN PRESTON

Willow Books
Detroit, Michigan

OXYGEN II

Copyright © 2025 by Beth Brown Preston

All rights reserved. No part of this publication may be reproduced, stored in a retrieval system, or transmitted in any form, or by any means, electronic, mechanical, recording, photocopying or otherwise without the prior written permission of the publisher.

Cover art: Aquarius Press

ISBN 978-0-9718214-4-6

Willow Books, a Division of Aquarius Press
www.WillowLit.net

Printed in the United States of America

CONTENTS OXYGEN II

Preface: The Crystal Room: Christmas 1963	5
The Gift	6
Still Life with Flowers—for Momma	7
A Poet—for Thomas Lux	8
Solo—for Michael Wintering	9
The Language of Love	10
Eye of the Storm: Ocala, Florida, 1914	11
Reflection	12
Zen #2	13
Memories	14
Anthropology	15
Broke Heart Blues—for DJP	16
Blind Love	17
Actual Proof	18
Scenes from Childhood: Cleveland, 1958	19
My Father, My Muse: Cheyney, 1959	20
Beauty	21
Birth of the Blues	22
Conversations with my Son	23
Descent	24
At the Library: Montreal, Quebec circa 1950	25
Blue: A Sonnet	26
An All-American Girl—for Gwendolyn Brooks	27
A Dream	28
A Theory of Devotion	29
Dark Kisses	30
Metamorphoses	31
Circles of Sunlight	32
Dawn	33
Marriage	34
A Rainbow	36
Red Earth	37
A White Rosary	38
Nefertiti	39
Memoir: Cleveland	40
Babyface: The Seventies	41
Descant	42

Berceuse	43
No Duerme Nadie	44
Wildfire	45
Infant Eyes (after Wayne Shorter circa 1973)	46
Moonlight	47
The Barn of Dreams	48
The Chanting of Dragons	49
Yukio	50
Bluesette	51
Invitation to the Dance	52
Collage—after Romare Bearden	53
The Painter	55
Childhood	56
Where Roses Once Have Bloomed	57
The Poet at Sixty	58
A Whisper	59
While I Was Away	60
Thunder and Lightning	61
Pride: Orfeo ed Euridice	62
A Windhorse Prayer	63
Lineage	64
Honor	65
Homage to Eric Dolphy	66
Three hundred sixty degrees	67
Dances with Ancestors	68
a. A Sleep Series/b. A Dream Series	69
River Walk	70
Inside My World	71
A Miracle	72
I Will Give to You My Heart	73
Inner Cycle	74
As Summer Fades	75
Emma's Song: A Lullaby	76
Charlie: Back Up Creek Road/Dandelion Wine	77
Landscape	78
November Separation: 2000	79

The Crystal Room: Christmas circa 1963

Christmas 1963: a photographic postcard in black and white
taken on the last Saturday in the month of December.
Momma dressed us up in our bright red chinchilla snow suits.
And Daddy snapped a picture of us standing close, gloved and booted,
two sisters holding hands at the bottom of our driveway.
We boarded the Pennsy at the Cheyney stop and rode into town
to Philadelphia's gothic Thirtieth Street Station.
Hailed a shining yellow cab uptown to Thirteenth and Juniper
and the magnificent edifice that was the John Wanamaker department store.
Momma's favorite purchases were Estee Lauder perfume
and genuine silk Schiaparelli stockings.
For my little sister Alice and me she would choose pale blue
Evan Picone sweaters with matching tartan plaid pleated skirts,
and black patent leather pumps we would polish with Vaseline
every Sunday morning before wearing them to church.
We dined on the ninth floor – the Crystal Room --
where mountains of fancy baked goods filled transparent glass cases,
and an all-white staff of waiters and waitresses served us from the menu
without question or protest any meal we ordered.
We sat always at the center table beneath the huge prism chandelier
rainbow arcs reflecting in our water glasses.

We sat together at the center table tall and proud -- the first colored
to dine in that luxurious room. But secretly still I felt out of place.
'Cause we were black and everyone else was white
as if there had occurred some angry and purposeful
omission of our kind.

The Gift

I call this inspiration the gift:
when I awake with a poem ripe, a sweet fruit I can pluck
from midnight's fecund tree. I light the bedside lamp
and find myself, sleepless, awake and alone
on a drowsy island of wonder.
I anoint my ears with the balm of music's fragrance:
the rhythms of jazz echoing through my room.
I live in this house built on a foundation of dreams.
I hide within omens foretold upstairs in the attic.
I rise and turn off the radio,
seize my notebook and in contemplation the helix reveals
this gene for poetry bestowed by my ancestors.
Two o'clock a.m.:
alone in the attic
I crack roasted sunflower seeds with my front teeth
trying to recapture the revelations of a muse.
The muse is you and the quiet desperation for poetry you inspire.
I send up a thankful prayer
I know will be answered
by the ritual of a poem this night.
From where do they come?
These sweet dreams? These truths?
These gifts?

Still Life with Flowers

For Momma

"A good woman is not an artist by profession," Momma warned me.
"She does not waste time writing immature poetry while surviving
on the money she earns by dancing topless in a bar near Malcolm X Park."
"She educates herself, finds a good job—a teacher or librarian—,
and supports her husband and her children with the fruit of her career."
"When she retires then she can write novels and paint."
Momma cautioned me about the dangers of an artist's life
when in sixth grade I revealed that I wanted to write poetry.
I painted my first canvas as a high school senior:
"The Breast"—an enormous painting of my bronze right teat.

I never painted with Momma's skill:
the silent spaces between her flowers set them apart
as unique and lovely objects. She would seize her pencil or brush,
her instinct surrounding us with the rites of righteous imagination:
still life with fruit in a bowl
still life with flowers in vases.

Momma, I fell moaning from the mouth
of your womb calling my name a poet.
Now your canvasses remain so mysteriously alive
with memories of tulips, daffodils, and fleur-de-lis.

A Poet

> For Thomas Lux—February 5th, 2017

I wanted to be the moon to your sun.
My persistent vision is of you boldly strolling across
a hushed college campus one August evening
a summer breeze ruffling loose the collar and cuffs
of your carefully pressed white shirt.
You spoke to me eagerly without words, proud and erect,
regal of bearing, as you walked in the opposite direction,
concealing the emotion revealed on your face.
I still hear the plainsong chant of your melodious voice:
the echo of a refined music throbbing in my ears.
You were the poet after whom I named my second son.
Your imagination roamed the boundaries between good and evil,
poetry circling between life and death --
anointed and bathed in darkness or a pure white light,
your voice edged with a gentle and bittersweet satire,
a contrapuntal music, a point counterpoint.

I remember your final lecture: "The poet is a wanderer."
"The poet gestures from beyond the horizons of language."
"The poet divulges a personal cache of symbols
revealed to him in early morning visions."

You turned your strong back to me and disappeared
into the arms of twilight's chilling embrace.

Solo   for MGW

Dear Michael:

I have written to you one hundred passionate love letters.
Your friends say my letters are kept unopened,
thick in their envelopes, dated in order,
under the desk stuffed in a brown cardboard box.
But I know you carefully have read each one.

You are the muse who appears in my dreams:
dreams of discipline, improvisation, and song.
You who assumes the persona of companionship
When I am alone. You nestle within and fill my emptiness.

Dear Michael:

No matter how many journals I write
always you emerge as my teacher, my mentor, my sensei.
And the inspired verse journal feeding my poems
Never grows weary of first lines, nor metaphor, nor image.
I have written you one hundred entreating love letters.
I speak of a personal and profound ache.
Alone without you I weep crystal tears.

Dear Michael:

Your eyes are moist with forgiving.
Face framed with silver-gray hair
encircling your face, a wreath of smoke and stars,
gleaming filaments of light.

The Language of Love

"The most beautiful language is the one you don't understand."
                                        Branko Cegec

The language of our love is universal:
lips tenderly touching, arms entwined in embrace.
We speak to each other out of silence. Me?
I am the insomniac. My mind fills with thoughts of you.
I seldom sleep.

Ella's voice rings from my radio, lyrical and true,
soothing as the morning cup of herbal green tea.
I slice a ripe lemon, add two sugars to sweeten.
Your voice in my ear sounds charged
with the electric excitement
of yesterday's happenings.

Before I knew the struggle of finding someone to love.
Then loving you came as a midnight stroke of lightning --
the answers to my eternal questions. You gave me the solution
to the equations that lay in our hearts.

My friends ask me if I still love you. And I never lie.
Always I answer—"Yes."

This evening again I see the lightning, hear the thunder,
prelude to a midnight storm.

I drink from the sweet cup of our love.

Eye of the Storm: Ocala, Florida, 1914

My daddy's birthday, February 18th, 1914:
the cabin windows rattled and shook
with the coming on of a southern winter squall.
Wide and long the fields of cotton and sugar cane
lay fallow as sleep under a cover of black mud.
Deep fertile ditches ruined by torrents of endless rain.

From the kitchen floated the rich early morning aroma
of my grandpa Caesar frying dumplings and slabs of pork bacon.

In the back-room Grandma Mattie was birthing my daddy.
The midwife rolled her sleeves, pulled down thick stockings
from her heavy blue veined thighs. Her strong arms arched
over Grandma's heaving aching belly.
She tucked a sharp blade under the shuck mattress:
"Mattie, a knife will ease the woman pains."

My daddy entered this world in the eye of a winter storm.
His head burst forth first like a ripe mango followed
by the body wet with dew and blood.
His first cry louder, more insistent than the whining wind,
or the staccato wail of a conch shell with news of his birth.

Thunder groaned and lightning cut the morning sky.
The infant was left to suckle on Grandma's breast.
She named her newborn "James."
Gazed into his innocent brown eyes.

And in his eyes the reflection of winter storm clouds.
And in her ears the clatter
of hailstones bouncing on the tin roof,
the sound of rain descending
like a chant of dragons.

Reflection

Since the cruelest sunset of your passing,
I have become my own closest companion:
enlightened by the wisdom of our years together,
moonstruck each lonely midnight by the love we once shared,
my thighs still heavy with desire for you,
my ears echoing the lyrics of our favorite songs.

Bluesette! Bluesette! Bluesette!
I'm cryin' the blues over you....

In a dream there was a garden where roses once grew.
Lotus flowers blossomed from the dark swamp of a pond.
Above the garden a magnolia tree shed its pink velvet blossoms.
Melon and moonflower graced this paradise.
On my lips remains the print of your soft sullen mouth.
And when I take a square pocket mirror from my purse
to make up my face in its reflection, in the mirror shines
the reflection of both our souls.

Today I dropped the mirror.
It fell and broke into many pieces--
Too many to collect or repair.
Without our reflections I was again alone,
my shattered soul on shards of useless glass.

Zen #2

I remember escaping from school for the second time in my brief twenty-year life. The first time I ran away from my Quaker boarding school. But this time I went AWOL from my college campus. I took a Greyhound bus north to Rochester, N.Y. My destination this time a Zen monastery and retreat located ironically within walking distance of the bus station.

When I arrived, the priest welcomed me with a friendly embrace. I gave him the small amount of money I had brought with me for lodgings and food. The initiates fed me warm bowls of brown rice, sliced tomatoes, and sugarless cups of an herbal green tea. Our one meal a day was served in the evening after a long intense day of meditation. We ate sitting on our futon pillows while an incense burner released a heady fragrance into the spring night air.

I've shed a million tears looking for love. And a healthy kind of love is what I received from the Zen collective of wise men and women who showed me how to squat in the lotus position on a woven straw mat quietly for hours. And when they thought I had mastered my mind they pinned a black narcissus to the collar of my blouse.

Nights I spent alone in my room dreaming one hard bop dream after another and whispering softly a windhorse prayer. I took a vow of silence. A vow like the one I once had made with a lover—that we would wed, and the children of our union would be born geniuses. But I broke my vow.

Later that week the priest told me I was not welcome in their world. That the reality of family and a formal education was calling me. And that voice was louder than any other. Someone in my family generously wired me bus fare.

And I returned to the saha world of mundane desires.

Memories

Daddy was a very handsome gentleman:
"a Geechee image of actor Clark Gable," Momma would say.
Six feet tall and slender as the fence rails dividing
our yard from the farm behind our house.

A dream man for a dreaming gal:
clear-eyed, intelligent, close to genius. Stubborn. Determined.

When the University of Chicago turned him down for a doctorate degree
he followed his North Star up to Montreal, Quebec, enrolled
in the university there and immersed in philology.
Penned his dissertation on Grendel in the ancient tale of Beowulf
while converted to Catholicism and rooming with a priest.
Considered becoming a negro priest, but instead decided
on marrying my mother.

Cleveland, Ohio: July 14th, 1951, they were wed.

Cheyney, Pennsylvania:
A child of six, I sat behind his English literature class,
lectures on Shelley, Hawthorne, and Wordsworth,
Robert Browning, Masefield and Tennyson.
His words would inspire the most innocent college boy or girl
to become a poet, a painter, a teacher.
Strict as a yardstick. Disciplined: classical music only on Sundays,
private piano lessons. Our first jazz concert: Thelonious Monk hammering
home his hip solo compositions on a worn Steinway grand.

At Northwestern U., Texas A&M, Fisk, or Cheyney:
Each day of his life spent educating Black youth,
leading them one step closer to destiny.
And when you asked him what he stood for he would answer:
"Education" and "our rights".

I still can hear his voice urging me to carry on his legacy:
to end my silence, to speak my truth.

Anthropology: Hiroshima
For Aiko

August 6th, 1945

Orange sky, black rain:
On the way home, thirty minutes from Kure to Hiroshima,
I heard through the trees, sirens scream and wail.
On the clear August day before, white leaflets fell like gifts
from the sky, warning our people not to leave the city.
They fell in paper clouds the citizens ignored.
We held hostage no American POWs.
We were the innocent victims of an endless rage.
Today people release hundreds of paper lanterns on the Motoyasu River
beside Genbaku Dome written with calligraphy
bearing the names of our dead.

Orange sky, black rain:
"Little Boy" falls from the Enola Gay into the morning sky.
The force – twenty thousand tons of dynamite.
The target – Aioi Bridge.
One hundred forty thousand perish in an instant.

Orange sky, black rain:
Overhead the flash of a strained lightning violated
the morning. In my ears the roar of thunder.
I, Kiyoshi Yoshikawa, covered my eyes and trembling fell
into a ditch as the searing heat of one hundred morning suns
scorched my back and spine.

Orange sky, black rain:
August 3rd, 1951, six years later.
I, now hibakusha, opened a modest souvenir stand
Near Genbaku Dome and sold penny postcards of Hiroshima
on the day of the atomic blast.
Now seventy-five years later,
people fold
one thousand paper cranes, drop them
from our tallest buildings and pray for peace.

Broke Heart Blues—for D.J.P.

"I'm worried in my mind, I'm worried all the time,
My friend he told me to-day, that he was going away to stay,
Now I love him deep down in my heart,
But the best of friends must part."

—Blues by Mamie Smith

You know my man done left me.
Wanna hear the news?
You know my man done up and gone.
Leavin' me with the broke-heart blues.

You know his skin was the color of honey.
Hazel eyes the color of dawn.
His skin was smooth as honey.
Eyes the color of dawn.
I gave him all the love I could,
but now he just up and gone.

I got down on my knees fore him
to beg and plead.
You know I got down on my knees fore him
to beg and to plead.
But his was the coldest heart
I ever done see.

Ladies if you ever see that man of mine again.
If you ever see that two-timing man again.
Tell him I'm still home waiting,
waiting just to be his only girlfriend.

Blind Love

for Steve

I want to write how I feel about you today:
Your quiet indignation at my leaving you so long alone.
Eleven months having passed, we are one year together in July.
I need to write of our hesitation in avoiding the inevitable.

Because of your confidence, I now fully believe in me.
And your spirit the motivation urging me toward the sacred.
As I sit on my bed in this musky June light, I carry inside
The seed of your promise, the antidote to all ruin within me.

Fear of separation leads our generous steps toward each other.
You are love's strict discipline. I am love's gracious mood.

Someone sleeps in the next room.
Someone who teaches me how to love you.

Our passionate cries echo throughout twilight.
We entwine in embrace as vines clinging.
You pull me closer, away from the reign of fear,
Away from our carnal distances.

In the next room on a table sits a vase of roses.
You and I will live inside each other forever.
The roses will not live. They will perish of fear and desire.
The roses will die of melancholy:

To hear a teardrop in the rain.
To hear a teardrop in the rain.

Actual Proof

for Steve

Prove the love one uses to penetrate the impenetrable.
As in the Japanese myth of the General Stone Tiger:
a man whose mother was eaten by a giant striped tiger.
In a rage for revenge, the son hunted the animal
until he came up on the beast crouching at the forest's edge,
or so he thought it was the tiger. And with his bow arm taut,
let fly a single arrow into a boulder mistaken for the tiger.

His arrow pierced impenetrable stone.

Prove the love one says to ask forgiveness.
My prayer for you, my lover, is a prayer of forgiving.
Forgive me that so long ago I let you run away
into the dangerous forest of forgetting.
And consumed by memory you disappeared from me
as if to a place inside the tiger's mouth.

Scenes from Childhood: Cleveland, 1958

Morning glory. White trumpets hanging on slender vines herald each city dawn.
Wet dresses stretched on backyard lines flap with the sound of starlings' wings.
The yard overgrown with red and pink roses behind our large, stately house.

We awake to the smell of Grandma's homemade buttermilk biscuits
and warm syrup.

On the long way down to school, carried aloft in Daddy's strong arms,
In the wind. The wind blessing brown faces for miles.
I learned to smear with paint my fingers on clean white paper,
To create my first, simple works of art.

And in the dancing wind. The wind in my hair, as I stood alone,
Weeping in the empty schoolyard, crying for Daddy to take me home,
Crying for the thought of wandering alone up those menacing streets.
Then he comes for me, regal and tall, to bear me up again in his embrace.

The wind. The wind sings to my breath, my life.
Father and daughter. Together we are one:
We are on the way home.

My Father, My Muse: Cheyney, 1959

I sat in my father's Freshman English class, the back row, Biddle Hall:
Wordsworth, Tennyson, Browning, Dickens became their college muses.
My father could inspire any innocent negro youth
to be a painter, a teacher, a poet, a master of sung verse.
He translates the name of Wordsworth to mean:
"the worth of words," and I laugh at the simplicity of understanding.

Outside the tall windows, angry bees swarm above the rosebushes.
Chrysanthemums explode into autumn's brilliant flame.

My father awoke in the common person some mysterious, childlike intelligence.
I loved to wander among the ancient volumes of his library:
Shakespeare, Moliere, Ibsen, the Greeks in translation.
I turned the pages of every book, a king's ransom of wonders.

Dressed up in academic robe, the ribbons of scholarship decorating his sleeves,
he appears in my reveries as a man of pure faith, a man of God,
speaking the worth of proud words, a cadence of memory,
a legacy, the substance of our souls.

Beauty

How do our eyes speak of beauty?
Beauty was born in a lonely Chinatown hotel room
where I dreamt of a thousand love letters.

Dolce, dolce, dolcissimo.
Soft whispers of your passion delight in my ear.
With gratitude I acknowledge your every complaint:
"The year was not quite enough long." "December has arrived."
"Each month ended before our essential tasks were done."

We test the spirited weight of our language.
Strong as your muscles, with permission to feel the pull, the heft,
our bodies are lifted to the skies.

Sunlight breaks against the walls of our room.
Soon someday this room will be emptied,
and our voices echo from these bare walls.

No one listened to me unless I sang.
Less I gave up to them a kind of vital music,
or spoke out of our sleep's nearly forgotten dreams,
or danced.

You captured me before we fell.

We always will triumph said my final letter:
our love will prevail.

Birth of the Blues

Was it Miles Davis' "Kinda Blue" bringing me home to you?
Or the musical memories of our mutual histories?
Scott Joplin and Jelly Roll laid back and fingering those piano keys,
on an instrument played by Langston Hughes, Bontemps, Zora Neale and Countee Cullen
while Black women danced a close sweating two-step
with their men in Harlem jook joints?

Were the blues born on sultry evenings under canopies of stars?
Come into this world between dark southern thighs
while our enslaved ancestors danced to strumming banjos,
wailing mouth harps
and ancient rhythms of violins, tambourines and drums?

Men and women dancing to words become songs:
work songs
praise songs
kin songs to the blues?

Were the blues born with the birth of "The New Negro?"
or "the flowering of Negro literature"? Or were the blues
more hidden, ever more subtle in the eyes and on the tongues of Harlem?

In the lyric of Billie Holiday crooning "Strange Fruit" at Café Society?
Or the crackle of Louis Armstrong's voice?
    or the clarion call of his trumpet?
Was it in the unstoppable Trane: a love supreme flowing from his horn?
    or in a Black child's first giant step?

Black man, my lover, I held your newborn in my arms
wondering just what he would make of this world,
a world he gazed on with sad, irreverent yet innocent brown eyes.

Black man, my lover, do not ask me
how you will survive without the blues.

Conversations with My Son

You tell me the Age of Fear begins that magic year – 1978:
same year your daddy parades around Greenwich Village
singing and dancing his own dark musical poems.
Your daughter is four. Sees in you that same dark magic.

There is a certain stillness about you tonight. A tough calm.

I hear your voice hovering over the distance between us.
Now the distance is my age measured by all these humble years,
the time of certain decline, cataracts like pearls in my eyes, slow limping
of gait.
Your daughter has learned to count numbers,
to spell with her private alphabet.
Numbers no longer matter to me now,
as if age is just another word for tired, so tired.

You forgave the years of pain: trauma, love and lies.
Did your daddy ever really love me?
Did he ever really love himself?

And you, my son, at age forty-seven, steps forward
accepting all the worship due a grown man with your kind of wisdom.

You say it is the Fear, brought on by time,
ravaging all within us like a heartache.

Descent

The silences interrupting the weighted silences
on the eve of your spiraling descent down the front stairs.
Awakened to your muses, you claimed to feel beside you,
on the floor, someone softer than the kiss of harmonies,
gentler than the melodies' denouements.

The difficult music of a dilemma:
What is flight? To soar aloft and never to return?

The unlucky fall. The falling, the stairwell steep,
onto an unfortunate bed of glass. Then blood everywhere.
Your descent serene as Icarus descending –
so quiet, so calm. Down the stairs and into the threatening darkness.

So Icarus' flight became a dare, as he dared obey Daedalus,
the urgings of his father to conquer with wax wings
a piece of silver-blue, cloudless sky over Crete.

Did you dream the birds were your only friends?
Did you soar beside warbling blackbirds?

Only you knew the feeling of flying too high.
Your wings broken and useless as you tumbled down.

Before you know flight, you must know ascent.

At the Library: Montreal, Quebec circa 1950

Portrait of a Black man as scholar among ancient volumes:
Abandoned by his native country for Canada,
followed the North Star to the destination of his mind's bright freedom.
His desire to write of the slaying of monsters:
"Then Beowulf spied, hanging on the wall,
a mighty sword, hammered by giants, strong and blessed
with a powerful magic, the finest of all weapons.
But so massive no ordinary man could heft
its carved and decorated length. He drew the sword
from its scabbard, broke the chain at its hilt.
Then savage with anger and desperate
lifted the sword high over his head
and struck Grendel dead with all the strength he had left…".

And the Black man wandered that library's dusty corridors
in a sacred building nestled on Montreal's steepest hills
gathering the endurance of mind to conquer his task:
to render the poem, so early it was sung only to kings,
a ballad, written by no one knows, yet passed on, in tradition,
glorifying the fierce and brave deeds of a warrior.

And the Black man himself became a warrior,
wielding the sword of language, fighting the good fight,
who basked in the light of a certain fame,
never worried about the consequences of his bravery,
save his own honor, of greater value than any poem.

The Black man rendered dreams a world without monsters.

Blue: A Sonnet

He asks me for a song, so I sing one just for him.
I sing of these unholy gifts stolen from within
the refuge of a music. A pale moon loiters
among the geometry of stars. They know about us:
Together joined under the white moon's angles of light.
Gossip spreads like shards of broken glass at our feet.
We stroll along the harbor of another night without sleep,
a festival of dreams awaiting us on the other side.
My song seems to fill with other poets' more generous.
They know of us: the way a simple riff rules our evening moods,
or the tattered silences between us. Each night
a quiet desperation. The stars measure the breadth of my love.
I cannot be for him whom I never have been.
I will wait for him…

An All-American Girl—for Gwendolyn Brooks

Topeka, Kansas, June 7th, 1917

Keziah:
Our baby girl's birth was not an easy one. She lingered low
inside my womb for days and nights. Stubborn. Defiant even.
Willfully against a world she someday would come to know.
The midwife and her sister arrived singing to comfort me
sweet gospel hymns I recalled from those church Sundays.
"Push. Push." My baby girl loosened her grip upon my womb
and entered this world squalling up a storm, telling us of her own pain.
David and I, we named our baby Gwendolyn Elizabeth—the tigress, the fierce.

David:
I hear Gwendolyn's voice at birth coming on strong.
We wanted her to own her mother's gift for music,
hoped for the songs already to live inside her, to imitate the sound
of Kezzie playing Mozart or Haydn on our old upright piano
while she floated in the waters of her belly.
My poppa never lived to greet his grandbaby, my father,
a brave man who fled his destiny of chains and slavery
to join the Union Army and fight in the Civil War.
Poppa would have been so proud of our infant girl.

Keziah:
Washed clean of my blood, she nursed at my swollen breast,
lapped the milk of our songs. Baptized in holy and sanctifying grace,
at home, sleeping in my arms, she seemed to know all wisdom.
Gifted of a thought deep and wide as the waters of the Kaw
or the watershed of Shunganunga Creek, she was moistened
with our kisses as we celebrated her born day, already knowing
whom she might become—so beauteous of regard, so righteous of language.

A Dream

Where the snow blinding, white lay cross the fields so thick and deep
we could step thigh high into a drift and the sharp red glint
of a redbird's wing flashed above our bowed heads.
Or while jogging up the mountain road one night during spring thaw,
our eyes barely perceived that dark place at roadside
where a grizzly shebear spied our footfall from the shadows.
Up the mountain path to our cabin nestled on a hillside
where all the simple dreams of life came true.
On the woodstove fire a kettle warmed to a shrill whistle
while the wind circled tornados among the leaves.
And where we watched, very still, through the open doorway
as the black shebear crouched on hind legs beside the creek teeming with trout
scooped out the helpless fish its blue gills trembling with death.
Where you stripped me naked in the chill,
wrapped my shivering body in your heavy lumberjack shirt
and a ragged flannel blanket. Too frozen to make love
we brewed tea. Cracked teacups filled with Earl Grey,
the comfort of warm liquid spilled onto our china saucers.
Our souls came to reside in those woods:
to grapple in the silence of growing things—
the trees added each a year to our own brief lives.
Where no one knew what secret we were withholding
from those below in the valley more broken who dared not dream.
Where we huddled together in the night beyond speaking.

A Theory of Devotion

In summer the garden was all she knew,
and the blossoming flowers of her several griefs:
skyblue Shiryuko Iris, Ki-ren Jyaku – the double flowering hosta.
She looked them all up in his encyclopedia of lonely days.
Love and despair were all she had but for the garden.
She walked among the daylilies – Heaven and Nature Sings,
singing those mournful Sunday hymns passed on down
by her grandmother. And taught by that woman's holy care,
a generation of long agos, she learned to cherish those seeds,
the time of planting and rain and love. Hers was the First Blush
as he took her careless among the hosta. Her naked brown bottom
held tight against the moist earth in summer rain.
His was not a gentle hand, but the voice of kisses and promises:
Onyx and Pearls she would possess if only she would remain
inside his kingdom. So, she let down her hair.
And now in his absence, she strolls among the green memories
down the garden path. Her womanly duty recalled
as the titles of books on his shelves. As the daylilies sway
in the breeze, her grandmother's legacy of love.

Dark Kisses

The distant warble of a Japanese flute.
We prayed and prayed, and our fervent prayers
brought down torrents of winter rain.
We are no longer sapling youth.
We have circles of new growth rings like giant sequoias
    or pine trees sweet and sticky with resin.
There is strength in our love.
Unbending like the pines' thick lower branches.
I write you frequent letters stating: "Yes. I still love you.
As you are my entire world."
But this world refuses to be stilled.
Its pulse beats with the rhythm of your captive heart.
We have grown closer by measuring our quiet distances.
This poem will be a valentine:
I love you as if I am an animal caught in your barn of dreams.
Within your embrace, you gently shape my body.
The evening sky is a confusion of starlight.
Dare I come to you in sleep?
Dare I disturb your dream?
We kiss under starlight.
Our kisses the gift to our dark, dark souls.
And for this dream, I feel no remorse, no guilt.
Only a chance to live within your power.
And for this love, there can be no reproach.

Metamorphoses

The elegiac cries of children's voices:
up in the north meadow where the wild horses graze.
Brazen with curiosity, we followed the stallions,
    eager to know instinct, their habits, their contemplation.
Why did the mares turn their heads so to gaze at us,
    young girls who like the mares could not be tamed?

Now we are grown. But the brown foals still wander in the meadow,
    or so they tell us, the offspring of those wild creatures.
We have become soft but muscular, sexual, unafraid of the wind
    that speaks of gathering storm clouds.
We desire a return to the north field,
to the land you have spoken of so tenderly,
to smell ripe clover and pluck the blue asters.

We are no longer children.
We are the changelings.
We have been transformed.

The pebble path up to the north field is black with tar.
New houses recently built surround the barn.
The time of then has become now.

And yet still we dance with the young foals in the meadow.

Circles of Sunlight

Spring arrives bringing circles of sunlight,
and bicycle wheels, blessing the afternoon breeze,
sunlight reigning over all these lengthening days.
I have taught myself to live with passion,
in the cadence, the revelation, the way.
Forest and hillsides are alive with blossoms and new green.

I write these poems for the sake of my children –
to let them know every little thing is going to be alright.
And their fear of time passing is without sanction.
For time is a strict and exacting mentor
asking merely the day's labor and a bittersweet perfection,
the task known only to brilliant sunlight and to the eternal wind.

Spring offers a season of choice: to wander familiar avenues,
or retreat into the forest of unknowing
under rays of sunlight inside a clearing,
the wide space between the trees,
where one may rest and breathe the fresh, liberating air.

I have made up my mind to poetry, a bird singing, to love,
though unreturned, a love that sings the body to open,
the spirit to open, and sings to the forgiving heart.

Dawn

The gray sky opens to reveal
A candy-colored orange cloud.
Sunrise is a poem full of metaphor unto itself.
I woke hours earlier at 4 a.m.
I love to watch the shadowy earth
Rotate ever so slowly and gradually
Submerge into a bath of eastern light.
I rise before the rest of the household,
Ready to shower and dress.
This is the sacred hour of prayer—
And I save my morning energy to chant the mantra.
From under dawn's thick cover of clouds
The golden sun peeks out.
Robins venture forth onto the front lawn.
Their heads nod curiously as if they might hear
Worms crawling through the damp ground.
The grass is wet with a glaze of hoarfrost,
Each drop sparkling a crystal tear of dew.

Marriage

                        for Otis W. Brown, Jr.

First there was that run in with the law in North Carolina.
You served your time down south
and bounced back to New York City.
Your zen moved you south again
from the bosom of the Big Apple into my arms.
You brought with you Chico, your calico cat,
an ancient leather suitcase full of poems in draft,
a change of clothes, and the clothes on your back.

We first met while you were poet-in-residence,
while you were surrounded with an audience
of astonishing beautiful and intelligent Black women.
But I was the woman who waited calmly in the wings
for you to look up from reading your poems
and to know just who you really were.

Late nights you wove tales of life in Greenwich Village:
adventures of you and your mentor Tom Weatherly
who clerked at the Strand Bookstore while you shined shoes.
And friends: Sue Childress (the only white woman
you ever slept with), Anne Waldman, Patti Smith,
Bo Breeden, Marty Watt, the chef Frank Wooten,
and the elegant Sandra Chapman who visited us
in South Philly only to make me jealous.

You told us how Wooten taught you to cook
restaurant style without burning your knuckles.
And Weatherly taught you the craft of poetry:
the simplicity, the authenticity, the rhythm.
Poetry was the other profession you learned
to practice with extreme caution and sincerity.
"The poem must flow with music," you insisted.
But the person you were to become
mixed your passion with desperate violent anger:
a lethal combination of emotions.

Yet I remember your tenderness,
and the quiet murmur of syllables and kisses,
the midnight roar of our typewriters
and the creak of the old bed
as together we fell to.

A Rainbow
for Miss D.

We were driving along the parkway headed for home.
Our talk about the music blaring from the radio.
Raindrops spattered the windshield with a spring shower:
Then came a rainbow!

We talked about the good old times:
When she came to visit my house
To prepare a special dinner.
We rolled sushi and baked a vegetable lasagna.

I thought she wanted to be my slave.
She was so fragrant with cocoa butter, soap & yogurt.

I wondered if any man had ever known her.
She needed to be worshipped like the Blessed Virgin.
And, since I too needed that worship,
I could do no more than surrender.

She walked strong and proud as the sun,
Still living in my conscious at that morning hour.
Her slender waist and staccato hips
Moved in magic rhythm.
For she was such a capricious coquette
The pleasure of being loved was her pride.
She was no man's slave.

Her sun soaked the city saffron yellow:
Parallel and blinding
the illuminating rays.

Red Earth

My voice speaks to you in Spanish,
An entire conversation, all the words in that language I know.
It is a sin not to remember deaths.
These poets now are dead: Gabriela Mistral, Silvina Ocampo,
Winett de Rokha, Yolanda Bedregal de Conitzer,
Claudia Lars, Carmen Alicia Cadilla.
Sisters whose eyes have closed with impatience, delirium.
These poets were taken from you and me,
Sent down into black tunnels of despair,
Become insomniac angels hovering over others' dreams,
Over cloisters, over fields where cows wander.
It was impossible to carry enough light into their rooms,
The illumination of their ache and wonder.
I loved their faces, women poets,
Reeling with knowledge of sensuality,
Their medusa hair ends of verse dangling, dangling.
What is this light that speaks from the terror of the past?
I am pulled backward, as in a half-sunken fishing boat,
Moored with my rope to the sagging wooden dock.
A young boy swims beside me in the lake on fire with sunset.
The earth is red and good.
The red earth cradles him in its womb of yearning and blood.
The boy is rescued by sense and sound. Perhaps, the end
Is in this line of angels defining manhood and womanhood.
All I now know is defensive, horrible.

A White Rosary

for Thomas Lux

A white plastic rosary, pale and polished,
Curled like a worm waiting on the night table,
Beside the bed, is my gift to you,
In the event of my death.

Also, to be found on my night table
An album of recent photographs
Taken of my sons and a calendar of angels
In memory of our mutual departed friends.

Ah, I remember one cloudy and restless Ash Wednesday
Witnessing the bold tattoo of charcoal
Across your forehead beneath your curl of white hair,
Your white hair gleaming in the early morning light.

As a child I possessed a similar white rosary.
Beads fashioned of quartz with the body of Christ
Crucified on a tiny silver cross.
Faithfully every Sunday my family attended Mass.

Finally, when I renounced my father's religion,
At the young age of twelve,
Much to his disappointment, I refused to tell him
Just how much I needed confession.

I feared the priest hiding in his shadowed box.
I did not want to tell him of my strange desires,
And my sensual, haunting dreams.
But Father told me to recite ten Hail Mary's in contrition.

And so, my rosary for which I no longer had any use
Disappeared into my mother's black lacquer jewelry box.
I hope this present of a cheap, plastic rosary
Will please you when I am gone. And, for you,

This gift will assume eternal value.

Nefertiti

for RWL

No one but I know the secret remedies,
My friend, the love potions,
The magic ingredients, the rich formulae.

From a far distance the morning horizon
Is all pale light and meringue clouds.

Astronomy:
You stir your breakfast coffee with one hand
& prove a theorem with the other.

Bittersweet black goddess within me:
A sense of sadness sweeps through our mornings
Like a cyclone. And even that melancholy song
Plays for us on borrowed time.
Whatever I now mean to you
Represents a series of profound encounters.

In my dream, I am doing seventy-five
In a fifty mph zone like some reckless
Self-satisfied diva acting out her emotions.

This bold black goddess within me:
Keeps me alive and real,
Exploring unknown territory—
The taste of salt on the tip of my tongue,
Grainy with language to season
The food of our memories.

Memoir: Cleveland

I remember the silhouettes
Cut from black paper and covered
With oval wooden frames and glass.

And I remember the man whose skilled hands
Sliced the paper until our faces appeared.

Those silhouettes hung on our bedroom wall:
One picture of my sister and one of me.

The sunlight burned bright after the storm.
The sky gleamed with paper heaps of clouds.
A jet stream divided the sky in two.

I awoke in the dark of early morning
To escape my dream of despair and pain.
There is hope in recalling our childhood:
A glimpse at first light, the world we loved,
Leaning over the edge of paradise.

Now someone holds me close at sunrise.
His beloved arms a circle of shelter around me.

Silhouettes: faded shadows on the wall.
My heart sings like a bird.

Babyface: The Seventies

I toil alone in the shadow of the darkroom
Waiting for the chemical mixture
To work its magic recipe.
Pale faces appear like mushrooms,
Taking on features slowly:
Eyes, a man's nose, a mouth.

A photograph of your face
Shows your generous smile,
Your visage bearing a gift of joy.

From infancy to adulthood
Your face never changed
From that first image which was captured
On film through the eye of the lens.
Your same smile illuminates my day.

You are shamelessly happy in the tintypes
Of yesteryear and boldly joyous
In today's fresh photographs
I have collected for you to see
Your handsome image.

I fit the new pictures
Into their clever wooden frames
For mounting on the bare walls of your room.

I was right all along about you:
You needed my help to survive.
The camera's nuclear flash
Gathered the light and your face
To create an image defying death.

Descant

One crystal morning we heard the song
Of starlings awakened and perched on the wires.
The pale blue light slowly surrounded and aroused us.
Leaves of grass turned over and spilled the dew.
I remembered the past seven years
Of emotion coursing between us
Like a steady current of electricity.

Next to our bed a radio played the morning news.
Then Nancy Wilson sang:
"An older man is like an elegant wine"
As we resumed the odyssey of our true love.
I say "true love" because the birds' song
Was a descant, an abstraction, a work of jazz,
A blues ode penned just for us two.

In one corner of the room my guitar slept
Nestled in its black case waiting for the caress
Of my fingers when I would take up my instrument
And reinvent the music.
Those same fingers of mine rustled
Your silver hair and stroked your forehead.

I keep a journal of all the feelings and the music.
Today marked just one more epiphany
As we celebrated the birth of this morning's dawn.

Berceuse

Thus would I have you familiar God.
Little flour wafer for the newborn child.
Wind and substance joined in exact expression
By love for the flesh which knows not your name.

    Federico Garcia Lorca

Our newborn in his crib lies sleeping in silence.
His delicate lips murmur innocent sighs.
I catch him up in my arms and gently rock him.
His tiny hands are balled into fists like unripe fruit.

The sky covers over the house with clouds,
And the rain descends in fine white sheets.
The sky is tattered with sulphur bursts of lightning.
The dark night answers one eternal question.
The nightingale warbles beyond the windowpane.

Safe inside we will not see the shadows nor feel the rain.
Our infant dreams through the twilight.

The road winds uphill all the way.
There will be comfort for all who seek.
The night's journey yields no resting place save home.

No Duerme Nadie
(Nobody is Sleeping)

Come lovely and soothing death,
Undulate round the world, serenely
arriving, arriving,
In the day, in the night, to all, to each,
Sooner or later delicate death.

"When Lilacs Last in the Dooryard Bloom'd—"
Walt Whitman

In my nocturnal and silent dreams
I witness the growth of green fields.
In a sleepless world of fecund streams,
I awake with desire for music in my ear.
Wind and waves achieve their solitary labor,
In every moment invading sleep.
Rushes brown tremble in their marsh beds.
Sunflowers are blessed by the goddess Persephone
With a glowing languor.
I cannot sleep.
I lay awake and pray.
I stand by the window peering out
Over the green fields and the trees' crackling branches.
Apple trees bend low bearing their burden for harvest,
And easily yield up their crop.

Nobody is sleeping.

Decorated in autumn colors
Furrows cross the cornfields.
Pumpkins sit on the barn's back wall.
Down near the stream, gently mirrored,
Ash trees hang over their reflections.
The wind is subdued and shivering
With the mountains' fall chill.
The trees' boughs arch through the woods.
Black branches of an ash climb toward heaven,
And to the light beyond.

Wildfire

A letter written by Edmonia Lewis addressed to the prisoner,
John Brown, in the Courthouse of Charles Town, Virginia.

October 17th, 1859, from the Oberlin Academy Prep School, Oberlin, Ohio.

My dearest John Brown, sir, news has arrived this far north
Of your final surrender into the hands of the lawless.
In the light of the moon, I often dream of you sir, my hero,
The gentleman who fought bravely with his sons at his side,
To liberate the enslaved of our western lands,
The good friend of Harriet Tubman and Frederick Douglass.
They say you believe as "General" Tubman—that all men shall be free,
No matter their color.

I fear for your safety, for your very life. Though I am born free,
I know the suffering of the Ojibwe people,
My mother Catherine's kinfolk, who were slaves,
Who danced in the forest, weaving baskets, sewing moccasins,
And embroidered blouses, selling their craft to the white folk.

I understand you, sir, because I, too, am wild and free.
I have wandered the forest, eaten raw fish, and swam beside she bears,
In the creeks and rivers of the Mississauga.
I, too, believe myself an "instrument of God."
We share a dream of freedom,
A dream for our people bearing no treason.
And I shall learn to cast in stone and metal
Your sacred face—an image that will last forever.
Yours in peace and freedom,
    Edmonia Lewis

Infant Eyes (after Wayne Shorter circa 1973)

Your perfect eyes full of grief and love gaze at me.
Your perfect limpid eyes are clear windows onto this woeful world.
You have captured me with your look of pure defiance.

People say it is not who you know,
It is what you know.

I have new knowledge of becoming,
the knowing of whom I really want to be:
a sacred brown woman singing my songs inside your strong arms.
You know the boundless hope that lives again and again
within the human heart, a bond for life, alive with healing.

Your eyes say this life is a journey we must take together.
So many worlds in your gaze, your eyes, your every gesture.
You know the cadence, the rhythm of our hips.
Your desire to see satisfaction in my grateful eyes.

You give me your love, silently, without words.
And in the silver silence of your message,
we rehearse the seed, the promise, the passion, the dance,
under a moon kissed sky of dreams

Moonlight

Some mysterious mood of light enters our window.
In the middle of our haunted dreams, we cry out loud
the love names we choose from a dictionary of myriad,
gleaming stars just above our bowed heads.

The blue night in conversation with every moving,
living being—our humble selves, our children, our animals,
and hovering over the graves of our ancestors.

Some holy beam of light descends from the heavens.
I behold your loving face in this holy stream of glow:
a kind of lucent singing against the glass of our windowpanes.
And inside our room, all is silence and eggshell white.
And I am a helpless witness to such beauty.

An owl's cry pierces the ever so deepening night.

Nestled under the owl's wing—a star.

The Barn of Dreams

Enormous the barn seems, almost a specter, a vision, or mirage.
The silo rising aside and above the gray slate roof. August.
I fell fast asleep in the hayloft.
Awakened under a white-hot sun, plucking strands of dry grass
From the damp curls of my hair.

What frightens me most about this landscape?

Up on the cemetery hill, gravestones gleam like bare bone skulls.
So much pity the wind is offering the cornfields below rippling,
and growing in the valley, yellow and green.

I believe my life might go on forever.
These memories hold all that I dare not forget.

The cows' bellows lament. Milking time. Udders full.
My horse tethered in her stall impatient stamps her hoof.
This farm, a chore, an adventure, an inheritance
from the legacy of my father. If only I could have imagined,
in my youth, he would pay me this one final attention.
Leaving this farm to my humble design. Old as Methuselah,
when the cancer took his last breath, he passed on to me a deed,
lettered on brown paper, tattered and wrinkled as parchment.

Sunlight eases the grief of life alone here.
But then appear the rainclouds!
This fertile loam is my best friend.

I will visit the place where my father is buried.
Today is just another easy day.

The Chant of Dragons

Deep in the village of Okumura, near Edo, in ancient Japan,
    during the time of drought, artisan villagers would fashion
    a paper dragon made of straw, sweet magnolia leaves, bamboo stalks,
    and parade the paper dragon through the countryside to draw rain.
And Nitta Yoshisada hurled his sword into the sea of Sagami
    to appease the rule of the dragon god there.
And Kino Tsurayuki threw a gleaming metal mirror into the sea
    at Sumiyoshi to tame the dragon guarding its waters.
And Bomo, the immortal god, hurled his staff into a puddle of water,
    arousing a dragon which came forth and carried him
    upward into the heavens.
Into the heavens the dragon ascended bearing the immortal
    upon the scales of his back: the three-clawed dragon of myth and lore.
What do we know of a world without seas nor lakes nor rain?
That the dragons have bestowed fertility upon the earth?
What do we know of the emperor who captured the dragons,
one male, one female, and trained them into obeisance,
so that he might govern wide fields of rich, dark loam?

A little black boy awakens from his dreams of emperors and dragons,
and wonders if all in his visions could be real,
or mere shadows of things to come?
And inside the quiet realm called his mind,
All the monsters were slain and down came the rain.

Yukio

A man is a tall mountain.
A man is like an ancient tree.

A man is like the sea: always retreating, ever returning.
A man is someone you never forgive.
A man is someone who shares with you a piece of the sky.

His body carries the weight of your memories.
Nature is listening to the song that I carry.
He should have been listening too.

We wished for a day of "the real thing": poetry,
Not those stuttering guns and flourishing hate.

We lay beside the ocean wearing only the white sea foam.
He gave me moments of silent reverie.
The lowing of a distant flute welcomed the dawn.

Who will listen with me to the cry of the mournful music?
Who will gaze with me at the music of the clouds?

Bluesette

for Steve

You do not have the answers to all our sweet names.
But I have loved you since on my doorstep we first met eyes.
Came the large defeat of a voice under my window last summer,
Telling me you fell three flights down your staircase,
And your wings were clipped. Meaning: both legs broken,
The bones shattered on the glass of so many broken bottles.

Until that time, our love was a kind of tyranny,
And became, after the tragedy, a dare no one could speak of
save you and me.

My heart and soul remain transparent as glass:
My love for you is sweet as water.

Invitation to the Dance:
American Sonnet

Now she sings, now she sobs in rhythm,
Sings a song becoming a spell, becoming a magic chant.
Hip-swinging dances of praise: hambone, rhumba, slow drag.
She moves with stately grace through darkness,
as around her gathers the blue-black blues,
awaiting her next gesture, her next moves.
String bass thumps a line, a tune.
She shakes to African melodies under soft hazy moonlight,
wearing a robe of many colors, she gently sways,
fingers shining with rings of silver and gold.
Her music's seduction echoes over fields,
and the wet ground shimmers under the rhythm of bare feet.
A woman of the universal dance:
She has become a creature of the moon.

Collage

after Romare Bearden

Gather out of star-dust:
memories of tender Harlem evenings where portraits filled
my young mind with jazz. And we stayed awake late nights,
in our rented rooms on West 131st, laughing and talking
the talk. DuBois, Hughes, Ellington. The gatherings
where I heard their stories, the abstract truth, scientific in grandeur,
yet ever so real, down to earth stories of Time and then,
the soothsayers, the truthsayers, singing their jogo blues.
Silence willfully broken. Scrapbooks of faded brown photographs,
clippings from Ebony and Jet. Folks dancing the original Charleston,
the fine old step, the swing and the sway.

Gather out of moon-dust:
There were crisis and opportunity. Black new voices, new forms.
Voices of folks singing out loud, or soft and mellow.
Lessons on how to become a "real poet," while Claude McKay
joined the Russian Communist Party. Fire from flint.
Letters were penned by Countee Cullen to Langston Hughes.
Shadows reigned over the evening skies of Harlem.

Gather out of sky-dust:
a time for the "new negro."
For Pullman porters to unionize
and for Josephine Baker, chanteuse extraordinaire, to float
on her wings of gossamer silk and satin.
Blues warbled from ebony flutes,
while poor folk sold their fine clothes to the Jews.
Was Christ Black?
Did angels really play trombones for God
in a black/brown heaven?

Gather out of song-dust:
Do we owe it all to Spingarn, Knopf or Van Vechten?
Or was originality and improvisation our sacred creed?
As I gazed from the windows at the skies

of my fading youth, all I could see was fire.
I wanted to hear the Blackbirds Orchestra wild on a Saturday night.
To hear "Go Down Moses" sung in church on a Sunday morn.
Wanted a style of my own.
To become Emperor Jones.
Daddy Grace.

The Painter

You sat with brushes in hand and the light flowing above and below,
a prayer like paper, the light illumined among all our sacred trees.
We forgot all our raucous and joyous other loves
when I asked you to listen for the screen door's slam
and the call to supper as I brought you the evening meal.

And then there was that folio of your recent sketches:
so many similar dark faces filled with joy.

Then I gazed at the rich, brown texture of a watercolor on the page,
a man's tortured face, his beard, his tough glowing bronze skin.
You said it was a portrait of your brother,
who died overseas during a rain of fire in the Viet Nam war.

And you put down your brushes to confess
we are going to start life all over again
without waging the private wars that keep us together.

You painted your dead brother's face
against a background of blue.

Childhood

Music became a halo, a birthmark, the praiseful signifying voice,
warning me not to live in the past, nourishing my young mind.
While rehearsing a sonata on the family piano, I forgot
the repetition of finger exercises, the scales, the tempo
on an otherwise quiet Sunday evening when no one was listening,
except my daddy, who thought of me as perfect; and he knew
each note to every song by memory.

             When I turned twelve
a backyard party entertained me with a stack of 45s, rhythm 'n' blues,
dancing, chilled sodas, and the sizzle of an old-fashioned colored bar-b-que.
A time for sprouting breasts, long, lanky legs, and knobby skinned knees.
While the Four Tops wailed their sweet soul Motown melodies from the
phonograph, I looked out from my bedroom window on the second floor
as fate come a-knockin at my door. It was all so right.

Years later, haunting memories of being twelve returned,
the ghosts of failure, with the music of unwritten songs in my ears.

And, my father, who once thought I was perfect, forgave me.

Where Roses Once Have Bloomed

Juneteenth, Galveston, Texas 1865

Where roses once were grown wild, she buried her departed dead:
their precious lives lost to a litany of chains and chokeholds.
Galveston, Texas, 1865: the anticipation and joy of emancipation
stirred the people to bold celebration. And yet, still not free,
she learned to speak in tongues and phrase they taught
from books as medicine for healing no one. Parades
of white Union soldiers rolled through the streets
with thundering bass drums, the rat-a-tat of snares, and cry of brass horns.

We claim the celebration today. We who are out here: so many brown people
come forth to relive those days when freedom was declared
to the march of General Order No. 3: "all slaves are freed" by Union decree.
But what of future generations? We walk together
in the footsteps of our ancestors while a new day is born.
The time for telling will again arrive.

Where roses once bloomed, she stepped lightly among the granite stones
over the graves of our Black Union dead and gently laid a wreath.

The Poet at Sixty

My life is a precious jewel.
Each day's worth far more than silver or gold.

I want to be a woman for this world.
And I keep on wondering just how I might possess
infinite love and compassion:
to be known for what I have freely given,
rather than for what I take from others.

True friendships have adorned my life.
I remember all the joys and sorrows,
the dues I paid along the way,
and the woman of grace I have become.

I have learned how to give and to receive love.
The seed of love planted within me grows.
My thirsty music drinks from the oasis of love.

My life is made of music.
My life is a song.

A Whisper

To wander the long, silent road under a cathedral of trees.
The ancient, tall oak whispers in my ear a tender farewell.
I have abandoned my former life. Why must I sleep?
Why not remain awake to think, then to dream of such sorrow?
The trials of love tempt me to sing of this.

Our house surrounds me in its loving embrace.
They say an old, crippled widow once lived in this house—
a recluse, shy, unknown among her neighbors. This Cape Cod house,
built in the Fifties, became her legacy for a grandson who lives down the road.
(He never lifts his head to speak, tending his blossoms as we pass by.)
The widow, his grandmother, long gone, but never forgotten.

A somber ceremony at dawn gathers us from our beds,
for steaming hot bowls of oatmeal, honey, walnuts and raisins.
In the day, our house, quiet as the rooms of a library.
Filled with children's bright laughter on starry evenings.

I think of the widow and know someday I will leave this place—
my books, a guitar, candles, prayer beads, my brown leather shoes.
All will be left behind as are those forgiven for their sins.
I have learned to want only the simple things:
I want to see the sunlight sift through the windows,
and falling between the oak trees.

In the afterlife, I will meet the widow.
What will she say about the past?
Who will she remember?
What will she know?

While I Was Away

The future came to pass while I was away in a dream.
And I returned home to ask what might remain for our children?
Would the polar glaciers melt into the sea and the waters rise?
In a world of unnecessary heat, would firestorms ravage the forests?
Would there be many winters without a trace of snow?

And then I awoke to witness the shattering of a country:
the common masses displaced, abandoned to wander without hope of shelter,
food or water. Hospitals bombed, houses destroyed and citizens hauling
their small possessions, innocent children, and their dead
on foot and in two-wheeled wooden carts.

I hear the cry of indigenous peoples everywhere!

The future came true while I was sleeping.
And I awoke to ask what would become of poetry?
Would I live to eighty-five and write many good poems?
Or would these verses be forgotten after my death?

The future arrived while I was in a dream.
I witnessed the seas rising, the forests aflame, a country shattered.

And I awoke to ask whether all this was as it should be?

Thunder and Lightning

The blue pulse of your gaze turned to lightning,
when first we met as prisoners of our own dark dreams.
Your eyes were full of lightning. Your voice echoed with thunder.

A crimson desert flower fades on the prickly cactus.
Lizards scuttle across the wide, dry riverbed.
Snakes coil against electric fences around the dying fields.

You gave me rain with the promise of your eyes.
And I dipped my tired feet into puddles in the yard.
The end of drought: a time I knew myself again, and you,
in the torrents of raindrops dancing on the sandy loam.

The desert flower blossomed once again.
The lizards swam in the current of blue, rippling streams,
and the fields were ripe with golden wheat and corn,
under the veil of gifted rain.

Pride: Orfeo ed Euridice

Love is stronger than pride.

In a cold, damp often lonely room in East London,
a young brown boy practices on his cello.
He dreams of playing for royals and presidents.
Music is his mystery. Pride reveals the music within him.

This young brown boy plays the soul of a Rachmaninoff sonata:
the third movement – a lyrical greeting to the gods,
and the fourth movement a cry of victory over all his pain.
And to his woman he offers endless, undying love.

Below the window, in the garden, his woman was singing.
She sang a blues to the water nymphs and fairies near the lake.
And bitten by a poison snake, beside the water she lay down to die.
The brown boy grieved and, in mourning, would not give his bride to Death.

So, he took up his cello and, on the wings of a Muse, descended,
to find his true love in the underworld. He spiraled down with music playing,
into the dark realms of Hades and Persephone, king and queen,
where the labyrinth was filled with the sweet sound of that sonata.

A promise: she might return to Earth following quickly his footsteps,
through the maze of caves. Carrying his cello on one arm,
the brave brown boy climbed the treacherous trail with her behind him.
But he looked back with pride to gaze into the eyes of his lover.
And she was lost, condemned forever to that underground Hell.

Love is stronger than pride.

A Windhorse Prayer

> I know time opens an apple seed to find a worm...."
> —Yusef Komunyakaa

Everything is possible in poetry:
This is a prayer for the energy of wind,
becoming life force and future, a measure of time
and seasons. The benevolent wind carrying aloft mantras of healing.
The flags are dancing in the wind with their holy inscription:
"May the merciful rain fall and bless our land."

Our music resounds within this windhorse prayer.
But is there time enough for a prayer to be answered
by a distant and forsaken God?
There are those who still walk in the light.
And there are others who live in darkness.

There is a specter haunting America that is us.
Our Black souls are magic at the center of this haunting.
We live in moments of truth or lies,
in this broken time that opens the apple seed to find a worm,
that separates a people from their history.

Yet, I know the eight winds will carry us back home:
whether in prosperity or decline, disgrace or honor,
praise or censure, suffering or pleasure.
Faith and fortune will come to us all.
And history will bear forth our songs.

Lineage

for my great-grandmother, born c. 1858

Dear Virginia:

Do you feel time pass in the afterlife?
Do you know how old you are even in death?

Almost to the day I was born, in 1953, Crick and Watson
found the structure of the DNA molecule – the double helix,
a polymer spiral, two strands wound about each other,
one spiral held to the second by a hydrogen bond.

The double helix is a ladder to the heavens, to the stars.

Childhood was the hardest act to follow
in the world of my dreams for this great granddaughter.
My pride was found in knowing you, in how I too was born
of your soul, and from the souls of your parents,
our ancestors with unknown names—slaves in Alabama,
circa 1850, bound together with chains.

This is our lineage: writers, painters, dancers, historians of the moment,
and this solitary woman speaking her poetic voice. We narrate stories
of our different selves for history. And we imagine your anger,
Virginia, you, dispossessed of children, of home, and gods.
Yes, there is history. But there is also inheritance:

In your flesh and blood, and in our sacred bodies
your beauty and dignity survive.

Honor
Frying in the Pan of Promise—Requiem (2017)
for Otis William Brown, Jr.—July 22nd, 1949 – September 9th, 2001

I was not beside you to hold your trembling hand at sunset
as one final, weary breath left your body.
But our son remembers everything about that tragic time
of your early and unanticipated death.
You held onto your life until the very last moment
when you murmured your farewell to this world.

Straight outta Fayetteville, North Carolina you hailed,
crooning backwoods songs and bluesy verse
with a calico cat Chico and your poems in a battered suitcase.
Opening the door for Black poets everywhere,
you scat and be-bopped cross our great country to San Diego,
where you bought me a wedding ring of turquoise & silver.

As a poet you were ever so human.
From you I learned lessons in the rhythm of poesy.
Heard epic tales told by the African griot inside you.
You sang melodies to me, sweet & lyrical,
while you burned knuckles on pans of black-eyed peas and ham hocks
in restaurants from Philly to the Big Apple.

And, as blue shadows faded into purple evenings,
we drew close in celebration of the music in our bodies,
the music of drums, saxophone, keyboard and marimba.
With your dark kisses you were my forever prince,
giving me the gift of language and courage.

If ever there was unconditional love,
you, selfless, gave your all. And that is why I now dedicate
to you this requiem. Since even when blind, love was our guide.
Because you taught me the language of our bodies,
on nights anointed with sweat and tears.

A country boy and a country girl.

Homage to Eric Dolphy: Love Suite

"When you hear music, after it's over, it's gone in the air.
You can never capture it again." —Eric Dolphy

Paris, June 1964

You have lifted me up to the light. And, on your sudden arrival
in Paris, I sensed a new day coming at dawn.
Your serenade – something sweet, something tender.
A passion song my heart and soul always will remember.

Our eyes met at Le Chat Qui Peche, in the intimate twilight
of a lonely table in the back. You stood proud on that stage,
before a crowd of noisy Parisiens, cradling an alto sax,
a naughty boy, tempting me with your horn's wild music.

And while you climbed the scales of a new composition,
we imagined a night of love in a cozy room above the cellar,
before one "Last Date." And I remember Madame Ricard's
smile as she led us upstairs. Charlie Mingus was there with his band,

on rue de la Huchette, in the Latin Quarter, thumping his bass
to an abstract tonal bebop. Every tune was love.
On the left bank of the Seine in June, I danced a ballet
of celebration to your flute sounds in the darkness.

What force removed you from among us? A vengeful God
who viewed our love as sin? The dance, the music, the jazz
was all innocence. A memory now. And I say to myself:
"It was all worth it"—our empty shoes beside the bed,
one sultry summer evening at Le Chat Qui Peche in Paris.

Three hundred sixty degrees

April 8, 2024

Eclipse:
Our beautiful sun hid by the sister moon.
Shadows spread across the fields like the music
of popular love songs. We gaze at the sky as the dark
overcomes our redeeming sun.

One hundred couples in southern Arkansas marry
in the time and space between darkness and light.
Honey bees return to their hives nestled among rustling leaves.
The Phoebe bird begins her mournful cry and, paused
on the branch of an ancient oak: "All is forgiven," is her song.

As day turns into moments of night, we witness for ourselves,
perhaps with new clarity or insight, a promise winging toward us,
hushed as daylight disappearing behind the moon.

Dances with Ancestors

...on the coast of Ghana, circa 1793

The Door of No Return

On those first fierce nights of our capture,
I slept with my head 'gainst my woman's breasts
in the darkest corner of the Cape Coast Castle.
Stone floors crimson wet with flowers of our fathers' blood.
The bone white moon cast a warning beacon over the ships.
The million stars above winked back their silver tears.

On those dangerous nights when first we were brought
to lie face down together in chains, I tasted blood on her lips
in one last forgiving kiss. The purple sky bruised with shadows.
As, in other rooms, gold and silver and ivory, taken from our land
to seduce our minds, waited to fill the decks of their boats.

On those sultry nights, before we were herded down to the ships,
I cradled my woman in a final embrace, placed my head
'tween her thighs, and on her belly full of child, my son
who never knew us, snatched from the womb, drowned in mother's blood
in the hold, on the middle passage in deep Atlantic waters.

On that foreign night, when last I gazed upon the soil
that bore me and my people, my heart bursting with sorrow,
I cried farewell to drum, to flute, and feather,
knowing my feet would never again dance
to the songs and tales of my ancestors.

a. A Sleep Series

I wake each morning at two, when the dark fruit of my poetry
seems to ripen, and the fields of the world lie fallow in sleep.
There is no turning back toward dream. Yet I know
of other dreamers who lie close together within their arms.
This is how the dreamers breathe – sharing one bed.
Upstairs the children are asleep, learning the new language
of their parents' naked love. I take up a blank white paper.
I witness the sky's black curtain glittering with stars.
This is the kind of nocturnal life I live.
Then Death arrives with the moon, a solemn visitor quiet on bare feet.
Why do I love this poem just before dawn breaks?
As the jealous sun climbs onto its celestial throne,
the pale blue sky melts into the brilliant hues of day.

b. A Dream Series

The pale blue sky melts into the brilliant hues of day
as the jealous sun climbs onto its celestial throne.
Why do I love this poem just before dawn breaks?
Then Death arrives with the moon, a solemn visitor quiet on bare feet.
This is the kind of nocturnal life I live.
I witness the sky's black curtain glittering with stars.
I take up a blank white paper. Upstairs the children are asleep,
learning the new language of their parents' naked love.
This is how the dreamers breathe – sharing one bed. Yet I know
of other dreamers who lie close together within their arms.
There is no turning back toward dream.
And the fields of the world lie fallow in sleep.
I wake each morning at two,
when the dark fruit of my poetry seems to ripen.

River Walk

twilight mythologies of sunset:
an evening walk along the river.
a woman wanders there alone, sobbing,
arms purple with berry stains and root.
she has read all the modern black poets
and, emaciated with her own knowing,
a victim of the eyes' bright starvation,
at home, she fills her shelves with nightmares,
the bad dreams for her daughters who languish
enjoying a brave new ending
to the novel of another important day,
upstairs on pillows fat as army cats.
her sons embolden with age like horses,
eager to abandon her barn of dreams
to make friends in the meadows.
but the stroke of a grandfather clock echoes,
with the woman's faint worried steps on the driveway
down to the country road following the river's petulant music.
"It would be good to be in heaven," thinks the woman,
"But better to walk down to the river."
a cascade of light sparkles across the water.
and now she feels her first freedom.
this is the way she lives:
a hydrangea bush on the riverbank is a haven of bright pink eyes.
into the water, she lazily dips one tired foot.

Inside My World

Once I remembered the rumble of trains
Groping their heavy trestle tracks into distances,
But time has yawed here. No way to smooth over
The passing hours into creases of time
Like wrinkles in a sateen shirt.
I choose a book, and the shelves move, tumbling
With an entire earthquake of knowledge.
And I will survive here until my lifetime has become
One sweating syllable I sing.

The bells are ringing in night's church spires,
And slowly the town is rocked down to the river.
The buildings lean, shadowed each, linking arms,
Making morose promises to the ever-thickening dark.
In a room with its ceiling rising skyward,
I write, on an elevator of light in which I am passenger,
To name the stars reaching for their ever more comforting heavens.

A stretch of white blazes across the nose of twilight's horse
As she gallops, races toward the museum's Greek pillars,
In an enviable flight toward all final departures,
Without conceit, scarcely reasonable, perhaps, along the path
Of chance in a paleology of these tedious last moments.
It is an hourglass I want to turn and turn again.

Out of the silent wreck emerges a song,
Slender as a young black girl.

A Miracle: Aubade

The night has ended and, o Lord, my eyes weep
At men not giving their all to aid this day.
The dark is drawing down, the forest bathed in light.
A choir of birds wake as the earth turns over.
Birds are singing everywhere as your tender eyes open.
You are the man who is tall straight and strong.
Who gives his seed till the smoke of dawn rises,
Who sings of redemption, redemption of the blood.

    We need this morning to open our hearts.
    The birds are singing of our love,
    And Fabrizio, my Fabrizio, you are caught up
    In my arms, the grasp of my fist, my palms
    Turned upward in an act of gratitude
    For our sleep, this hammer, has left nothing to dream.
    The helmsman turns away from his wheel.
    The slave turns from his oar.

We do not yet understand these first lisping words,
That someone would decipher from our madness
A theory of devotion. Our ship approaches the island.
But our secrets are not revealed until the fires of dawn,
When our unborn children wait in seed
Inside your sleeping phallus with a magic that makes us weep.
You are the handsome prince, Fabrizio, who endures
My attention, saving the gift of your soul
For this day, this poem.

I am huddled here in this cloud of memory.
You say that I am easily startled, and our parting
Is all my fault. The song lies in the bird's egg.
And you, my lover, awaits your time
To go forth into your children's arms.

I Will Give to You My Heart

I will give to you my heart
Because this is all I have to give.
My heart clothed in joy
And wildly beating with pleasure.
My heart full of ballads
And nights of hard bop.
And if you accept my gift
You will discover your life profoundly changed,
Into a life of goodness, kindness and warmth.
It is not an easy thing to give love.
But my love is like sweet music.
I will give to you my heart,
Still beating, alive with passion.
I have offered you love
That graciously you accepted,
Took my love whole and entire
A cherished thing that can be shared.
I will give to you my heart
To keep like a charm on a golden chain.
Keep my heart. Share my heart.
You will find boundless joy,
And eternal peace.

Inner Circle

As we journeyed north in the circles of our separate lives,
we crossed pathways like two newborn moons
within sky bound galaxies in the deep vast of the blue.
You came into my life with thunder and lightning.
And now that you are loved, as you should be,
we reach through the dark across the distance between us,
as the stars above lullaby the night,
my romantic warrior.

As Summer Fades

One morning when she cannot be wakened,
Clouds will rest softly on her eyelids
Exactly where she wants them. Her hair will languish
Upon the pillow. Two bodies, hers and his, rolling
Hard against each other. She dreams as the birds' song falls
Towards her window. It is a final exodus: the summer fades.
Her slumber is heavy as a hammer's descent on the head of a nail.
She dreams in the crosslight of worlds, between minutes, seconds,
In the spare time and space of a reverie.

His body moves closer warming her sweat,
Two souls brewing their dank teas.
A cry breaks from his chest. His lips taste the salt
Of her back. If only they never would wake.
But an elixir of light fills the window—
Shedding its bright glow on their brown faces.
The clock's eyes watch them measure their newborn hours.
As summer fades they wake and rise
With the gentle fog that dresses morning.

Emma's Song: A Lullaby

You are soft and sweet as this season.
Soft sweet summer in Manhattan, New York City.
Your precious face wears a serious gaze
Telling us you are here to envision your own world.

A painting by your gifted great-grandmother hangs
On your nursery wall. She was a woman of hope
Who loved all children. And I do love you, Emma,
As a child who needs my love.

Who will you become five, ten, fifteen years from now?
Will you be a poet, a musician, or dance the ballet?
Will you be a leader who helps us set right the course of this world?
I see the future in your shining eyes.

Emma, your birth was the answer to my prayer
For someone small and warm to adore.
You are light as a feather now.
Someday to be a heavyweight woman of no small consequence.
Grown and learn, Emma, learn and grow.

While you sleep, the entire sky yawns,
Its vast black mouth twinkling with stars.
Sleep, my pretty one, sleep.
Here come your tomorrows!

Charlie: Back Up Creek Road/Dandelion Wine

How quickly the seasons of this sanity disappear.
I cannot bring your world to life as nature herself paints.
Silent, so silent as maiden nature I toil
Beside the dimming candle that drops its ladders
Of wax from a window of bright lights.
I see before me all the days that will follow,
The days when you will bring to me
Sultry afternoons with swift violent showers,
The tiny hands of buds reaching
For the laughter in your face, blossoms gathered
Early to weave around my damp forehead,
Symbols of virginity and innocence.

I have kept a bouquet of dried faded flowers
Long beside my bed, and my lonely bed
Becomes the wide field wherein you sleep with me.
And this is your world of waves that ebb pushing
Stones gently along the creek bed.

My hands are never still. With courage I paint for you
A never-to-be forgotten still life or a portrait.
I harness color for your sole attention.
Then life itself grows inside my body.
I am no longer even honestly slender.

I was haunted by poems that seemed to grow
From simple scraps of scarce paper.
Paper became so thin and matchless a medium,
I could fold whole flocks of birds while watching
Clouds revolve around your rooftop.
While other lovers wrest their satisfaction from knowing
Their lovers lived solely for their own sake,
Yes, I must admit that it was all in vanity
To be caught with you showing off my inelegance.
Fashionably late for dinner. Fond of the engraving,
But not of the invitation.
Flutist at the wedding, but not the bride.

Landscape

Push me forward in a wheelbarrow!
For God's sake, let me watch the black smoke drift
Back and forth from the rooftop chimneys.
Let an owl cry loud in my ear,
And the bells of night's lost people ring out
With their merciless regrets. Moment by holy moment,
May a child's voice recite the day's beatitudes
While a nun in silver habit waits and silently listens.

Bring twilight to me, to my very arms, my bed
Wherein I must behave like a spinster queen
Pardoning her twice-married consort.
This is all I ask of the hour before sleep:
The promise of lightning in the air, the stars
Rising with the gentle fog that dresses the night.

Push me forward in a wheelbarrow, O my God,
Toward every possible evening blossom.

November Separation: 2000

Because I wanted to write this valentine
And my words were composed on cheap yellow draft,
Since there was little more than electricity,
Paper, pencils, not a sign of new books,
I wanted you to possess these poems, a boxful,
Yes, these poems in the kindergarten tongue of dead snakes.
Here they are, curled and waiting:
An extra set of teeth, a chain drawn
Across the mind before sleep
On the night of Schubert's birthday.
As one century slips away, it is good only
To remember those sad months, the far distant
Country, the empty elevator one forgot
To slam shut, the gold hoop earrings
From the homeland.

We brought those gifts, for every man and woman,
Our arms were filled with them.
And they cast them down like children.
They cast our presents aside, asking only
That their boxes be filled again.

In November, you were gone, sweet Daedalus.
You took off for another dominion of clouds.

ACKNOWLEDGMENTS

"The Crystal Room: Christmas, 1963" *South Florida Poetry Journal*, February 2023
"The Gift" *Black Art Magazine*, Summer 2024
"Still Life with Flowers" *The Courtship of Winds,* Winter 2023
"A Poet" *The Courtship of Winds*, Winter 2023
"Eye of the Storm" *Evening Street Review,* Summer 2023
"Memories" *October Hill Magazine,* Summer 2023
"Anthropology" *Arlington Literary Journal*, 185, September 2023
"Blind Love" *Storm Cellar,* Fall 2020
"Birth of the Blues" *Mid-Atlantic Review,* Spring 2024
"Conversation with My Son" *Potomac Review*, 74, Spring 2024
"At the Library" *Evening Street Review,* 39, Summer 2023
"Blue: A Sonnet" *Birmingham Arts Journal,* Winter 2024
"An All-American Girl" *Evening Street Review*, 39, Summer 2023
"A Dream" *Evening Street Review*, 39, Summer 2023
"A Theory of Devotion" *Black Art Magazine*, Summer 2024
"Red Earth" *Pennsylvania Review*, Fall 2020
"Nefertiti" *African American Review*, Vol. 46, Nos. 2-3
"Memoir: Cleveland" *African American Review*, Vol. 46, Nos. 2-3
"Descant" *Sinister Wisdom*, 115, Winter 2020
"Collage" *Chiron Review*, Fall 2024
"The Painter" *Decolonial Passage*, 51, Spring 2024
"Childhood" *Mid-Atlantic Review*, Spring 2024

About the Poet

Beth Brown Preston is a graduate of Bryn Mawr College and the MFA Writing Program at Goddard College. She has been a CBS Fellow in Writing at the University of Pennsylvania and a Bread Loaf Scholar. Her work has been recognized by the Hudson Valley Writers Center, the Sarah Lawrence Writing Institute, The Writer's Center, the Fine Arts Work Center in Provincetown and by A Public Space. OXYGEN II was a finalist for the 2023 Moon City Press Poetry Prize.

Her work has appeared or is forthcoming in *Adanna, African American Review, Atticus Review, Birmingham Arts Journal, The Black Scholar, Callaloo, Calyx, Cave Wall, Euphony Journal, Evening Street Review, Free State Review, Hanging Loose, Helix, Illuminations, Muse, Obsidian, Oyster River Pages, Passenger, Pennsylvania Review, Pensive, Potomac Review, Rain Taxi, Seneca Review, Sinister Wisdom, Storm Cellar, Talking River Review, That Literary Review, Vox Populi* and numerous other literary and scholarly journals.

www.ingramcontent.com/pod-product-compliance
Lightning Source LLC
Chambersburg PA
CBHW031428290426
44110CB00011B/571